BRICK

EDITED BY WILLIAM HALL

BRICK

ESSAY BY DAN CRUICKSHANK

BRICK

As a boy, I lived in a nineteenth-century Sussex farmhouse built from local Horsham red brick. One summer evening, as sunset turned the walls salmon pink, I noticed some darker two-inch-wide diagonal stripes across some of the bricks. These, my father explained, showed where the bricks had been piled up during firing. What I had unthinkingly considered a machine-made block, void of interest, was actually nuanced and preserved a record of its formation. Later that day, hours after the sun had gone down, I remember feeling the warmth held in our tread-worn century-old brick path. So bricks held warmth as well as history.

There's a comforting honesty to a clay brick. As well as reading its history, we can hold a brick and know its weight, its texture, and its composition in a way that a concrete wall is comparably unknowable. Its work is visible unlike stucco or a curtain wall of glass. And whereas limestone or granite are austere, grand and exclusive, brick is modest, unpretentious and inclusive. A brick is after all just earth – the humblest thing imaginable.

One of the greatest architects of the twentieth century, Louis Kahn, famously imagined a conversation with the material, asking, 'What do you want, brick?' Brick replied: 'I like an arch'. Kahn continued, 'Look, I want one too, but arches are expensive and I can use a concrete lintel ... what do you think of that brick?'. Brick says: 'I like an arch'. Kahn wanted his students to see the limitations – and especially the potential – of materials, and to use them appropriately.

Some of Kahn's exceptional brick arches are featured in this book (214), amongst other buildings that exploit and champion the material, like Sir Edwin Lutyens' graphic Grosvenor Estate

(124–5), Peter Behrens' breathtaking dyeworks (206–7), or the audacious, foreboding and transcendent Grundtvig's Church (284), which dispatches any notion that bricks are just for making houses.

No other man-made building material has been around as long as brick. And in the right conditions – such as those found in the Iranian desert at Tchoga Zanbil (336) – bricks can survive for centuries, so it's hardly surprising that some exceptional works of architecture have endured.

But this book isn't just about the past. It shows that today's architects are finding new forms of expression and have chosen brick for its various unmatchable qualities. Many of the projects utilise new technology, one of them (142) was built by computer-controlled robotic arm, and Wang Shu's staggering Ningbo Museum (352) – which merges found brick with many other recycled materials – demonstrates that brick is central to new ways of thinking about architecture.

It wasn't difficult to find remarkable brick architecture around the world, yet no illustrated books have been published on the subject for over a decade. This suggests that despite its ubiquity brick is woefully underappreciated. I think it is time to reappraise – or perhaps repoint – our view of brick. This is the place to start.

William Hall

THE FIRST CITIES

Brick is a wonderful material. I've pursued it around the world. There's an alchemy about brick – about all building materials made from fired clay – where the elements of earth and water are transformed by fire into a material that can be more durable than stone. Through fire, a soft, ephemeral and 'base' material – mud – is transmuted into the hard, the eternal, and the beautiful. Perhaps it is the beauty of bricks that is the starting point of my love affair.

Many materials can be hard – wrought iron, steel, or concrete – but they don't have the character, or the ancient pedigree, of brick. And as well as hardness, history, beauty and character, brick possesses great subtlety.

A brick's colour and texture is the result of the mix of clay from which it is made, perhaps with the addition of other materials, and of the manner in which it has been fired – primarily the temperature, length and regularity of the firing process. Also, unlike many other hard building materials, bricks breathe, almost as living beings. Their open cell structure makes them wind-proof but breathable, which means they are the ideal material for homes. They also offer superb insulation – helping interiors remain cool during a hot summer and warm in cold winters. Since they also function as heat reservoirs because of their high heat retention capacity, bricks can actively help warm a room. In a brilliant manner the heat stored during the day is gently released when outside temperatures fall.

The inherent qualities of brick, aesthetic, economic, environmental and structural, seem to have been recognized by mankind at a very distant time. Indeed, as far as it is possible to tell, bricks are the oldest man-made building material. The first cities made by man – such as Uruk in Mesopotamia which was founded around 6,000 years ago, and Harappa and Mohenjo-Daro in the Indus Valley dating from around 4,600 years ago – utilized brick and other clay products. Both these locations were near deposits of alluvial soil, which were ideal for brick-making, and the lack of timber or stone suitable for building meant that brick technology had to be developed. The bricks used in these cities were typical of early brick construction: both sun-dried and kiln-fired.

The Ziggurat of Eanna at Uruk, approximately 4,200 years old, is a good example of early brick construction, as is the now much-restored ziggurat at nearby Ur (174), that was started about 4,000 years ago. The core of the Uruk ziggurat is made of sun-dried bricks with mats between a number of courses to help level and sustain the structure while the bricks and the mortar in which they were laid became more solid. Over this core was laid a facing of hard kiln-fired bricks. And occasionally at Uruk, earlier and smaller sun-dried brick structures were faced with kiln-fired clay cones, of different colours and laid to form abstract patterns.

When I visited the ziggurat, I observed that the kiln-fired bricks had been mostly robbed long ago – and that the sun-dried bricks survived to a large degree and in generally remarkably good condition, although molten by the rains. This can also be seen in the ruined and mighty Peruvian adobe-built 'pyramids' – like Huaca Larga at Tucume (166), dating from around 1000 AD – that are so vast and weathered they look like part of the natural geological landscape.

What amazed me at Uruk is that the kiln-fired bricks were as sound as the day they were made. This put me in mind of what is now regarded as the world's oldest book, *The Epic of Gilgamesh*, written about 4,700 years ago. Gilgamesh was a king of Uruk who sought immortality and found it, ultimately, through architecture and the construction of cities wrought in strong kiln-fired bricks. Gilgamesh realized that his name stamped on hard bricks, 'where the names of famous men are written', meant that his creations and his memory would last for eternity. The kiln-dried brick was the passport to immortality, a guarantee that your creations – and your name – would live forever.

As I worked through the ruins of Uruk, everywhere lay fragments of brick, which prompted my imagination and proved Gilgamesh correct: he was alive in memory. Also, in even greater numbers, lay clay cones, in tens of thousands, and occasionally a small stub of cone-faced wall. When the dust was washed off the wall an enigmatic pattern emerged – chevrons, lozenge shapes and spirals. These are of course the patterns found on much later mosques and mausoleums, such as that of Isma'il Samani (264), Bukhara, Uzbekistan, which dates from the mid-tenth century and incorporates brick-built columns decorated with ancient abstract patterns – and also in Romanesque Christian churches, such as the stone-built Durham Cathedral. But here at the ruins of Uruk, I saw the origin of the mysterious and ancient sacred language of abstract forms rendered in kiln-baked clay.

There are many myths and mysteries about the origin of brick-making and brick construction, as revealed by the Biblical

Old Testament, probably written around 3,000 years ago. *The Book of Genesis* outlines the making of the Tower of Babel and records that the people said to one another: 'Go to, let us make brick, and burn them thoroughly. And they had brick for stone, and slime had they for mortar.' (Genesis 11:3). A fine description – burned brick 'for stone', but 'slime' for mortar has always puzzled me. Surely what is meant is lime, for cultures that learned to fire clay to make bricks also discovered that to burn and 'slake' limestone allows the manufacture of a fine mortar that dries almost as strong as stone.

The Book of Exodus tells us a little more about early brick manufacture. When the 'Children of Israel' were exiled in Egypt the Pharaoh increased their labour by refusing to give them straw to make their bricks (Exodus 5:12–14). So at an early stage straw was mixed with clay, which would bind sun-dried bricks and help as a fuel if the bricks were kiln-fired. This lack of straw provoked the crisis that resulted in Moses leading the Israelites out of bondage to the Promised Land. So, arguably, brick-making has much to do with the subsequent history of the world.

All these early bricks are, most sensibly, dimensioned to be held easily in one hand by a bricklayer, who would use the other to spread mortar. The exact brick dimensions can vary – most notably the depth – but the principle remains the same.

Those bricks used around 2,600 at Babylon, in Iraq, and on the ziggurat at nearby Borsippa are of familiar pale red-brown colour and dimension – but brick making technology had evidently been greatly improved with bricks that were harder and of more regular shape and size, and sometimes laid in bitumen rather than lime mortar. The technological revolution that had taken place is revealed most dramatically in the bricks used at Babylon to form the lower stage of the Gate of Ishtar. In their precision and technical sophistication these finely moulded and fired brick beasts anticipate clay-based terracotta ornaments, such as the figures in the 'terracotta army' made only a few centuries later in China – around 210 BC – for the vast necropolis of the 'first Emperor' Qin Shi Huangdi. These creations are, arguably, the ancient ancestors of the terracotta and faience decoration that enjoyed such a vogue in the later nineteenth century, notably in Alfred Waterhouse's Natural History Museum (140), London, of 1873 to 1881.

But although brick making in Mesopotamia had been greatly improved by the third century BC, an old idea lived on in Babylon. Here – and on the scattered bricks of the shattered ziggurat at Borsippa – I found many bricks stamped with the name of their creator, Nebuchadnezzar II, 'the king of kings'. He, like Gilgamesh, sought immortality through well-burnt bricks – and found it. Technology was again improved by the Chinese, who around 2,220 years ago were capable of making a vast quantity of bricks at high quality for the construction of the Great Wall (356–7). The Romans not only put brickmaking on a vast industrial footing but also explored its structural potential. The vast Baths of Caracalla (338), built in Rome between 212 AD and 216 AD, remains a wonderful monument to engineered brick construction. The strength of supporting walls comes not just through materials and bulk but also through design with, for example, the judicious use of relieving arches. These help to transfer loads and allow walls to be pierced with openings or sculpted with niches without being weakened.

Such buildings were part of a giant technological leap forward in the manufacture and application of brick. All brick-using cultures of the ancient world were carried along. For example, the Palace of Ctesiphon (50), Iraq, built about 540 AD by the Sassanid Persia retains what is – with its internal span of 24 m (79 ft) – the largest un-reinforced brick arch vault in the world. The 52 m (170 ft) high Malwiya Minaret (15) at Samarra, Iraq, built in 851 AD, is a superb and massive construction in brick, taking the form of a spiralling and gradually tapering ramp – a symbolic staircase to heaven. The sensational brick-built Kalyan Minaret (310) in Bukhara, Uzbekistan, completed in 1127 AD, rises 45.6 m (150 ft) and was anciently perceived as the tallest extant man-made structure and one of the wonders of the world. Like the Tower of Babel it was seen as an expression of man's audacity – almost a challenge to God's creation. In fact the minaret or Victory Tower at Jam (134), Afghanistan is – at 62 m (203 ft) – taller, but it was not built until c.1174 and was well off the beaten track. In fact, it was so secluded in a secret valley that was not discovered by the west until the 1950s. The Tower at Jam is not only a monument to the structural stability that is possible when strong bricks are used well (the tower stands on the banks of a river and in an earthquake zone) but also to the subtle beauty that is possible. The outer surface of the tower is decorated with Kufic lettering, rendered in brick, that proclaims the nineteenth Sura of the Koran with artistic perfection.

All this is history – but in many parts of the world traditional brick-making and use remains a living art. And this is what makes the exploration of brick architecture so fascinating. Shibam (242–3), Yemen, a city that dates back perhaps 2,500 years, is formed of towers, each jostling for space on a slight rocky outcrop above a riverbed and next to a desert oasis. Each of these towers – generally around six storeys high – is made from sun-dried wafer-like bricks formed from alluvial soil that is swept to the oasis each year by the river. Constant maintenance is essential, and when I was there, brick-making was in full swing with mud being mixed with straw in traditional manner, pressed into moulds, with the bricks then laid in the sun to dry. I saw a similar process in Djenné, Mali, where the Great Mosque (56–7) – last rebuilt in the early twentieth century – is the largest mud-brick built structure in the world.

In Europe the technology of kiln-fired brick construction was slow to match Roman standards but the fortress-like cathedral in Albi (40–1), France started in 1287, is a sublime essay in brick architecture. With amazing skill, the cylindrical forms of towers are buttresses that flow into walls and battered base to create a sculptural architecture. Its emotive power resides in the juxtaposition of abstract forms united by their brick construction.

By the late-seventeenth and early-eighteenth century English brickwork was arguably the best in the world. Lessons had been learned from Dutch brick traditions and developed. In England all the elements of brick construction came into play and were realised with harmony and perfection. Brick bond and detailing became of paramount importance – with Flemish bond favoured from the mid-seventeeth century with corners and window jambs quoined with quarter bricks called closers. Brick colours were matched and contrasted with a high degree of artistic concern – often red bricks for window dressings and brown or purple for walling. The crafting of details was important – even for humble buildings. Notably rubbed and gauged fine quality bricks were used for window arches where joints would be razor thin. Such high quality bricks, perhaps specially moulded to form architectural features such as column bases or capitals, could be used for the entire facades of high status buildings. Mortar mix was of critical importance, with ingredients and their proportions dictating colour, texture and strength.

And pointing was an art in itself, for example flush-pointing, penny-struck and tuck-pointing. The aim was always to make the joints neat and as narrow as possible, exemplified by the additions to Hampton Court Palace (36) designed by Sir Christopher Wren during the 1690s.

Brick continued to be a major building material throughout the world during the nineteenth century. Its strength, durability, availability and relative cheapness – and a beauty that improves with time (if somewhat homogenised when made industrially) – made brick unassailable.

Bricks were used structurally – as in the Maidenhead Railway Bridge, Berkshire, designed in 1839 by Isambard Kingdom Brunel. With its shallow, twin spans – each 39 m (128 ft) in width – meant it had the widest and flattest arches in the world. Similarly, the Monadnock Building (240), Chicago, is a pioneering 16-storey high-rise building, which was started in 1891 to the designs of Burnham & Root. Its outer wall is formed of load-bearing brick-work of great thickness, cladding a metal-frame. Brick is an ideal material in many ways for this type of building because of its compressive strength, fireproof nature and because it offers good insulation and is durable.

The twentieth century saw brick used as both a load-bearing structural material and, increasingly, as a facing material over steel or reinforced concrete frames, or as a veneer in cavity-wall construction. Its use as a mere cladding material can reduce the visual interest of brickwork, giving it a 'wallpaper' role; header and closers which indicate a solidly bonded wall are replaced by repetitive and economic stretcher bonds.

But memorable examples of brickwork were still achieved. For example, the load-bearing brick walling, with its Art Deco forms, over a steel frame at Battersea Power Station (332) designed from 1929–1934 by Sir Giles Gilbert Scott, and the sculptural, Expressionistic St Martin's Garrison Church (234), Delhi, of traditional load-bearing brick construction, designed in 1930 by Arthur Shoosmith. Louis Kahn's Indian Institute of Management (266) at Ahmadabad, built from 1962–1974 is another later, superb example: its elemental, Roman-inspired manner of poetic power and resonance only achievable in brick.

As this book reveals, in the twenty-first century brick continues to play a creative role in the making of sound, functional and delightful architecture. Indeed, in this age of ever-increasing concern over ecology, sustainability and energy conservation, bricks – with their long-life span and splendid insulation characteristics – remain an ideal building material.

Dan Cruickshank

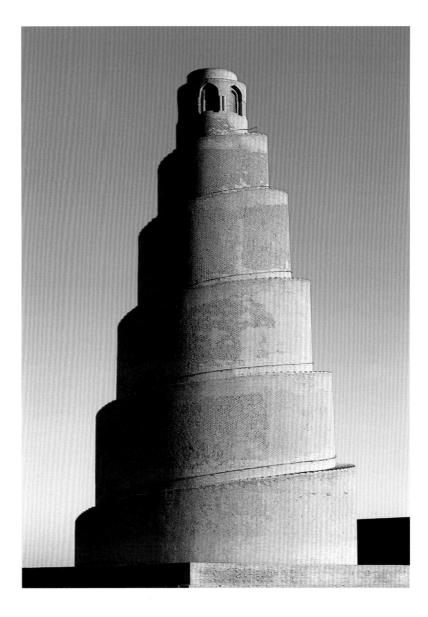

◀ Once the largest in the world, the Great Mosque of Samarra was all but destroyed in 1278. Only its outer wall and this minaret – originally covered in dark blue glass mosaic – remain. A spiral stepped ramp leads to the top, 52 m (170 ft) above the ground.
Malwiya Minaret, Samarra, Iraq, 851

Undulating 8 m (26 ft) high walls contain this single-storey college in a forest northwest of Bangkok. Using earth from the site, 600,000 bricks were made locally by hand – and by foot. The thick walls insulate the building from tropical conditions, while irregular apertures promote ventilation and offer places to sit.
Kantana Film and Animation Institute, Kantana, Thailand, 2011, Bangkok Project Studio with Boonserm Premthada

In an upmarket neighbourhood in New Delhi, rapid economic development has resulted in a collection of defensive and introspective homes. Architects Vir.Mueller were keen to create a new typology that is welcoming, firmly situated in the locale and references the area's built heritage – such as medieval Islamic architecture. Defence Colony Residence, New Delhi, India, 2011, Vir.Mueller Architects

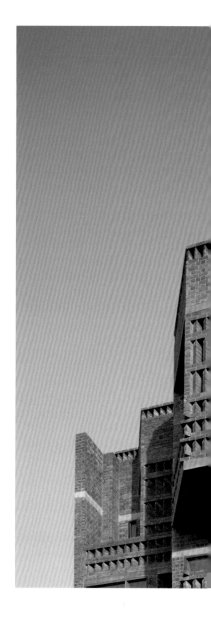

'If present day architecture is ever to mature, it needs to eschew the fashion of the hour and consider the realities of decades,' said Harry Weese a year after the completion of this church in rural Indiana. Skylights running the width of the roof illuminate apparently windowless spaces. The larger 'sanctuary' to the left represents the church, while the smaller building in the foreground is a chapel. Both surround an enclosed courtyard. First Baptist Church of Columbus, Columbus, Indiana, USA, 1965, Harry Weese

Inspired by J.S. Bach, and invigorated by a change to the Catholic Church's liturgy in 1963, Douglas Cardinal and his client, Father Merx, aimed to conceive a spiritual building as it might have been had basilica and cruciform models not been adopted. Apart from the vertical walls no element of the building is straight. The sinuous walls rise and fall depending on the space they contain, and billow to promote remarkable acoustics. St Mary's Church, Red Deer, Canada, 1968, Douglas Cardinal Architect

◀ These 22 m (72 ft) high towers have a curiously timeless quality that is part medieval, part industrial, part futuristic. In fact they were part of a coking site which covered 300 acres (122 hectares). Coke production creates large quantities of phenol, and the towers provided a water purification system. When the plant was shut in 1991, 15,000 workers lost their jobs. The site is now protected and open to visitors. Lauchhammer bio-towers, Lauchhammer, Germany, 1958

Kahn's sprawling government complex is best known for its monolithic concrete centrepiece, which contains the debating chamber. These collateral administrative structures have a similar form but are smaller and made of brick. National Assembly Building, Dhaka, Bangladesh, 1982, Louis I. Kahn

This small chapel provides a non-denominational space for peaceful reflection. Its cylindrical form and shallow moat create a visual and metaphorical break from the predominantly orthogonal campus in which it sits. The rough and varied bricks are defensive, yet soften the building's presence. MIT Chapel, Cambridge, Massachusetts, USA, 1955, Eero Saarinen

This exceptional niche, part of Wren's extension for King William III and Queen Mary II, shows the apotheosis of seventeenth-century rubbed and gauged brickwork. The technique requires highly refined, often sieved, clay to be carefully fired, producing bricks of an even colour and texture. These are then hand sanded by a skilled craftsman using a rubbing stone. A thin lime putty mortar assembles the work before a final sand across the entire area. Hampton Court Palace, London, UK, 1694, Sir Christopher Wren

This cheaply constructed country house – intended to be a model that could be reproduced elsewhere – is designed with simplistic construction details that allow unskilled builders to construct it. Neatly overlapping bricks express the building's triangular plan.
House 712, Barcelona, Spain, 2011, H Arquitectes

▶ Construction of this building – the largest brick cathedral in the world – took more than 200 years. The exterior retains a defensive military appearance as the building was initially planned as a fortress in 1282. Brick was probably used because no suitable stone was available locally in sufficient supply.
Albi Cathedral, Albi, France, 1480

This distinctive 18 m (59 ft) high brick-clad pitched roof provides scale and grandeur to an assembly hall that marries central European modernism with a Dr Strangelove aesthetic. One million yellow bricks were custom-made for the project. Federal State Parliament, Vaduz, Liechtenstein, 2010, Hansjörg Göritz

In a maze of medieval streets this tautly crumpled facade was borne from respecting sight lines and right to light laws. The strongly faceted cuts required that 25 per cent of the brick shapes used were made specifically for this building. The brick-and-void bond used here allows light to penetrate the walls, avoiding the need for larger apertures which would compromise the visual integrity of the angular form. Saw Swee Hock Student Centre at LSE, London, UK, 2014, O'Donnell & Tuomey

◀ This art and architecture park – the Museuminsel Hombroich – is on the site of a former NATO missile base. During a twelve year period, sculptor Erwin Heerich created eleven simple pavilions, invariably using reclaimed brick from Dutch houses. This example is one of the few structures in this book that is not made from locally sourced materials. Turm Tower, Neuss, Germany, 1989, Erwin Heerich

De Klerk's final work before his untimely death, this complex of nearly 300 homes is spread over 30 acres (12 hectares). Like his earlier Het Schip the building is a fine example of the Amsterdam School. The movement was related to the contemporaneous Brick Expressionism movement. The buildings, invariably in brick, are characterised by complicated, dynamic or organic masonry, and often imbued with symbolism. De Dageraad, Amsterdam, Netherlands, 1923, Michel de Klerk and Pieter Kramer

This brick arch – the only extant structure of the ancient city of Ctesiphon – is the largest ever built standing 37 m (121 ft) high and 26 m (85 ft) across. Originally it formed a roof that was 50 m (164 ft) long. Its heavy metre-deep (3 ft) apex required support from walls that are a staggering 7 m (23 ft) wide at the base. Taq-i Kisra, Ctesiphon, Iraq, 540

This Lutheran church sits on bedrock overlooking a suburb of Stockholm. A huge number of materials are used for a small site – green and white glazed, red, perforated, and lime washed bricks among them – yet their masterful composition and restrained detailing have resulted in a quietly powerful space. The walls are made of load-bearing brick, meaning the brick supports the weight of the roof and walls. This is unlike many of the later twentieth-century buildings in this book which have a reinforced concrete structure. One result of supporting such weight is that the walls at ground level are nearly a metre (3 ft) thick. Årsta Church, Stockholm, Sweden, 2008, Johan Celsing

53

After a self-imposed absence from architecture of over ten years, Lewerentz won the competition to build this church in 1956. Standard bricks are used throughout for walls, ceiling, and parts of the floor. Demonstrating his virtuoso control of the material, the bricks are always used whole, never cut or shaped. Spaces and different thicknesses of mortar are employed to add complexity to a standard module. St Mark's Church, Stockholm, Sweden, 1960, Sigurd Lewerentz

▶ The first mosque on this site was built in the thirteenth century. In 1906 the French administration arranged for the rebuilding of the mosque, though it is unclear as to the authenticity of the recreation. Constructed of plaster-covered mud brick, the building has become a cultural icon of Djenné, and of Mali. Great Mosque, Djenné, Mali, 1907, Ismaila Barey Traoré

This unconventional church eschews ecclesiastical convention, and perhaps signifies an abandonment of colonial doctrine generally, following Uganda's independence from Britain in 1962. A baptistery and choir, a chapel, and the confessional are each placed in one of three quarter cupolas – which in turn represent an African martyr.
Mityana Pilgrims' Centre Shrine, Mityana, Uganda, 1988, Justus Dahinden

Popularly known as the 'Lemon Squeezer' on account of its star-domed form, this Roman Catholic church is raised on a pedestal and accessed by a wide staircase. The eight wings are each enclosed with a parabolic arch. Böhm recognised the form as having 'overcome gravity', and considered it a metaphor for the resurrection of Christ. St Engelbert, Cologne, Germany, 1932, Dominikus Böhm

Dieste was a prolific and innovative builder, frequently making small structures and testing ideas. He was interested in creating architecture specific to the developing world. This thin shell vaulted roof and sinuous double-curved wall are a beautifully spare and highly economical solution to creating what is essentially a rectangular room – the shape of the wall contributing to its strength. Church of Christ the Worker, Atlántida, Uruguay, 1958, Eladio Dieste

This residential and office building for an association of 19 Christian denominations features two flowing recesses, each highlighting a staple of Christian ecclesiastical architecture, namely a bell and a cross. Ecumenical Forum, Hamburg, Germany, 2012, Wandel Hoefer Lorch + Hirsch

TEXTURE

◀ The names of Saints, Popes and other Christian luminaries decorate the exterior wall of this chapel in South America. They are arranged in chronological order with the most ancient at the base and what was the most recent – Pope John XXIII – at the top. The vertical positioning of some bricks belies the conceit that they are somehow part of the construction of the wall. Nonetheless the names appear to be part of the fabric of the wall, communicating a sense of solidity and history.
Archdiocesan Seminary, Montevideo, Uruguay, 1958, Mario Payssé Reyes

This summerhouse, on a granite island in central southern Finland, was used by Aalto as a test bed to explore the efficacy and performance of bricks in a harsh environment. It also offered the opportunity to consider the aesthetic effects of the bricks themselves, and of the impact of different jointing and bonding. Jointing is the term given to methods of finishing the mortar edge, for example with a flush, v-shaped, or concave joint. The renewal of this mortar is called pointing or repointing.
Muuratsalo Experimental House, Muuratsalo, Finland, 1953, Alvar Aalto

This open-air heritage museum is a collection of vernacular buildings from across the Netherlands. A 143 m (470 ft) long wall formed of bricks of different bonding and jointing methods welcomes visitors to the site – a clear nod to the variety of bricks to be found beyond the wall. Every horizontally laid brick has a long side – the stretcher; and a short side – the header. Bonding is the name given to the arrangement of stretchers and headers in the wall for the purpose of strength or decoration.
Open Air Museum, Arnhem, Netherlands, 2000, Mecanoo

Sáenz de Oiza was one of the most experimental and influential Spanish architects of the twentieth century, yet this small parish church is very little known. It is difficult to imagine the distinctive yellow brick bell towers having been inspired by any other material. St Michael the Archangel, Cadreita, Spain, 1959, Franciso Javier Sáenz de Oiza

73

◀ Built by Cardinal Thomas Wolsey, then gifted in an effort to retain favour with King Henry VIII, Hampton Court has been a royal palace since the early sixteenth century. There are 241 chimneys at Hampton Court and many are elaborately decorated to display the immense wealth required for their manufacture. These extraordinary examples are faithful reproductions of chimneys installed on Wolsey's original 1514 building. Hampton Court Palace, London, UK, 1514

Jujol worked as an assistant to Antoni Gaudí before designing this hilltop chapel. Built in the countryside between Barcelona and Tarragona, it was begun in 1926, but due to lack of funds was not completed until 1999. The bricks included an unusual mixture of limestone, charcoal and gravel from the nearby River Gaiá, giving them a grey complexion. The form of the building has repeating triangular clusters. The catenary arch interior – one example of the influence of Gaudí – is expressed externally in the form of the screened windows. Church of Mare de Deu de Montserrat, Montferri, Spain, 1926, Josep Maria Jujol i Gibert

This 50 m (164 ft) high temple marks the spot that the Buddha achieved enlightenment. One of the oldest and best preserved brick buildings in India, the tower was restored during the eleventh century, and again by the British in the 1880s. Mahabodhi Temple, Patna, India, 260 BC

Fusion is an Islamic cultural centre that unusually combines Turkish and Moroccan community centres and mosques in Amsterdam. Rohmer drew inspiration from Arabic architecture, and from local examples of Brick Expressionism to create a hybrid visual language that is specific to the building. Fusion, Amsterdam, Netherlands, 2009, Marlies Rohmer

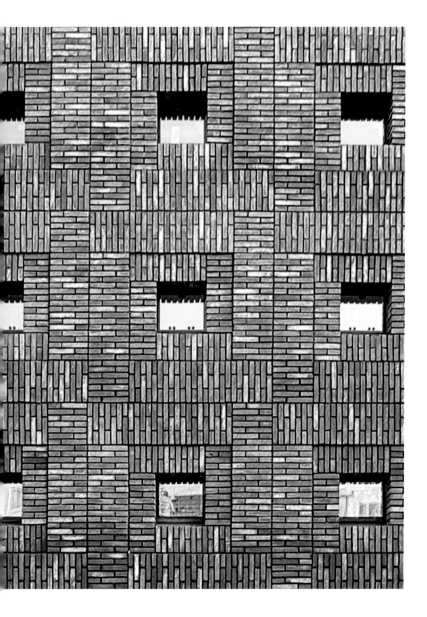

This windowless tower housing state archives is softened by a subtle shallow relief pattern. Different lighting conditions are heightened by the raised surface, giving the building a mutable and lively character. NRW State Archive, Duisburg, Germany, 2013, Ortner & Ortner

An activity centre and offices are incorporated into this social housing block of 170 homes. Like many contemporary projects in this book, the building is clad in brick panels. Cladding is the name for an external finish which is not structural. Here the cladding is underpinned by a reinforced concrete structure. The brick panels simply offer a rich tapestry of colours and textures and allude to the variety of local brick buildings. Block A Noordstrook, Amsterdam, Netherlands, 2009, Dick van Gameren Architecten

Constructed over 13 years, this continuous serpentine block of 620 maisonettes represents a radical departure from typical high rises of the same period. The eponymous wall itself, shown here, was intended to provide an acoustic barrier to an unrealised motorway, and to provide shelter and a sense of containment.
Byker Wall, Newcastle, UK, 1982, Ralph Erskine

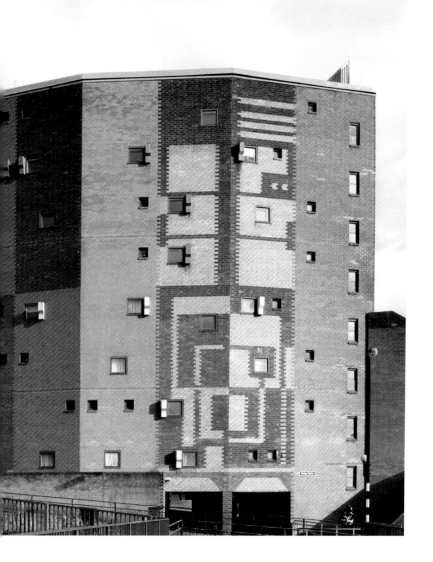

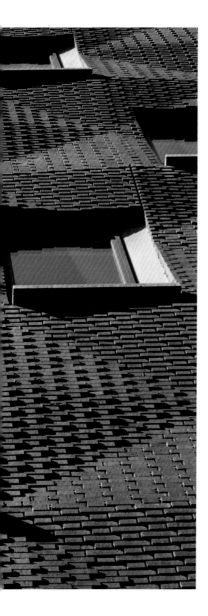

Local planning codes required that this reinforced concrete high-rise apartment block must be clad in masonry. To create the undulating brick facade, each panel was created off-site. A rubber form held the bricks in position on the floor, and concrete was poured on top. When cured the rubber form was removed to leave the monolithic panel ready for mounting to the facade.

Mulberry House, New York, New York, USA, 2009, SHoP Architects

89

This facade is part of a refurbishment to improve the energy and fire standards of an ailing 1960s building. The position of the billowing brick buttresses relate to an underlying reinforced concrete framework. Metallic grey bricks contribute a lively shimmering surface and marry with neighbouring structures: one, brick and the other, aluminium. University of Technology, Munich, Germany, 2013, Hild und K Architekten

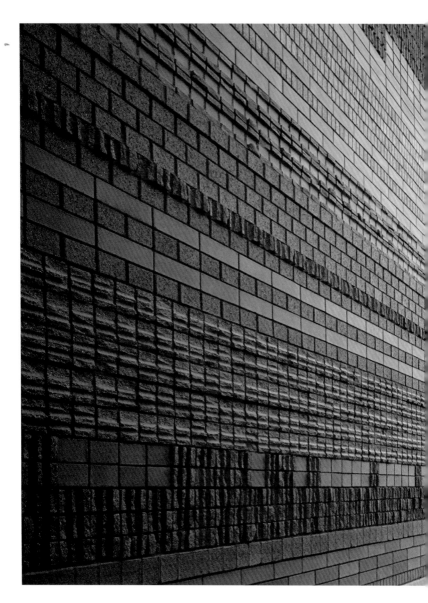

The architects of this university laboratory, m3architecture, wanted to express the relationship between creativity and science. They did this by treating the interior in a formal way with clarity and precision, and treating the external cladding with a more expressionist approach. Red brick was specified to relate to neighbouring buildings. Micro Laboratory, Brisbane, Australia, 2001, m3architecture

This building first served as a covered market, but was expanded in 1340 to incorporate meeting rooms for the city council. During this enlargement the ornate brick Gothic screen, shown here, was added. This exhibition facade, decorated with coats of arms and elaborate brickwork serves purely to elevate the majesty of the building and thereby demonstrate the wealth and importance of the city. Stralsund City Hall, Stralsund, Germany, 1278

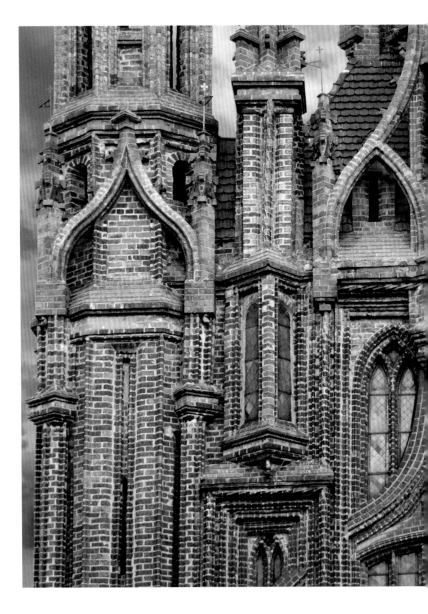

◀ A defining landmark of Vilnius, this Roman Catholic church is built in an intricate style known as Flamboyant Gothic. The elaborate facade is formed of 33 types of especially shaped brick, and has remained virtually unchanged in 500 years. Legend recalls that Napoleon declared a wish to carry St Anne's home in the palm of his hand: the romantic notion didn't prevent him commandeering the building for the use of the French cavalry. St Anne's Church, Vilnius, Lithuania, 1500, Michael Enkinger or Benedikt Rejt

Bigot, who studied and later taught at the École des Beaux-Arts, is best known for building an 11 x 6 m (36 x 20 ft) scale model of ancient Rome in plaster. His education and interest in historical precedent somewhat explain the elaborate brickwork of this Archaelogy Institute. The intricate detailing demonstrates how brick, which can be unwieldy and limiting, can be used to delicate and sophisticated effect. Centre Michelet, Paris, France, 1930, Paul Bigot

Building on a site with scant historical references, Aedes Studio created their own. Echoing many post-industrial cities across Europe, they conceived a former factory building, then imagined its conversion into modern apartments. This conceit – or perhaps deceit – allows for a series of engaging details, such as chimneys, metal cages for balconies, and apparently random positions of double height spaces. The whole remains coherent due to the consistent use of brick. Red Apple Apartments, Sofia, Bulgaria, 2013, Aedes Studio

Arata Endo was the first architect to share a credit with Frank Lloyd Wright after working as chief draughtsman on the Imperial Hotel in Tokyo in 1923. Built in a Mayan Revival style, these hotel buildings reference Japanese patterns and ornaments as well as themes from the earlier Wright building. Koshien Kaikan, Japan, 1930, Arata Endo

As in many of his buildings, Gaudí here employed a catenary arch to give this educational building style and strength. Other decorations display the potential of ornamental brickwork and Gaudí's virtuoso control of the medium. Colegio Teresiano, Barcelona, Spain, 1889, Antoni Gaudí

◀ Housing the ancient excavated remains of the old city, Moneo alluded to the Roman remnants by creating a series of arches clad in so-called Roman Brick. This term can refer either to surviving ancient fired clay bricks, or – as here – to modern day bricks, which are long and thin. Museum of Roman Art, Mérida, Spain, 1986, Rafael Moneo

A pupil of Antoni Gaudí, Martinell became a specialist in wine cellars – or wine cathedrals as they are proudly known locally. His work is spread across Catalonia but this is perhaps the most impressive interior. Using local materials the building observes recommendations made by the Catalan government of the period, voluminous aisles and well aerated wine reservoirs amongst them. Cooperative Winery, Pinell de Brai, Spain, 1922, Cesar Martinell i Brunet

This striking building provides off-site storage for the chemicals, solvents and compressed gases required for Humboldt University. Some of the equipment for that purpose can be seen in the glazed turrets. Visitors can be in no doubt that this building has a special and perhaps dangerous function – one suspects even insects avoid it. Hazardous Material Storage Facility, Berlin, Germany, 2004, Benedict Tonon

Several colours, and some especially fabricated bricks with an embossed woodgrain impression, are carefully arranged to convey the effect of a timber facade on this home for the elderly. The arrangement of small-scale detailing demonstrates the potential for this complexity to soften the appearance of a large building. Mornington Nursing Home, Victoria, Australia, 2007, Lyons Architects

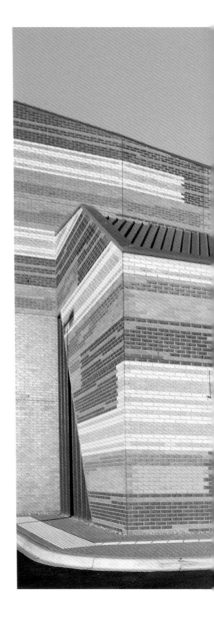

JUXTAPOSITION

◀ This 76 m (249 ft) high tower houses 148 km (92 miles) of shelving behind its windowless facade. Rising up from the grounded walls of a 1930s corn silo, the new building is clearly demarcated by the change in form, and by the elaborately patterned brickwork.
NRW State Archive, Duisburg, Germany, 2013, Ortner & Ortner

Built on a sloping site, this modest island community centre incorporates homes, shops – many of which have since been converted into council offices in accordance with Aalto's long term plan – a library and council chambers. Aalto created a Finnish vernacular building, replete with sauna, which is unpretentious and of human scale, yet communicates the dignity and architectural tension of much grander equivalents.
Säynätsalo Town Hall, Säynätsalo, Finland, 1952, Alvar Aalto

These tiered offices are sited on an industrial estate. This environment, coupled with the client's paternalistic approach to its staff, led Wright to create an introspective building, centred on a large open plan, top lit office space. Externally, the fashionably streamlined and curvilinear forms promote the organisation – a pharmaceuticals company – as utterly modern. Wright designed over 200 different shaped bricks for the interior and exterior brickwork.
Johnson Wax, Racine, Wisconsin, USA, 1939, Frank Lloyd Wright

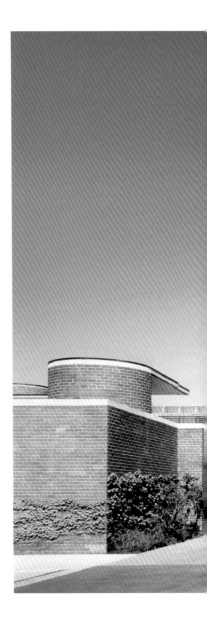

This otherwise foreboding structure is softened by its lively brick facade, and by numerous intricate details integrated into the brickwork. Inside a single top lit space 30 x 25 m (98 x 82 ft) provides intimacy between the priest and congregation. Sadly, the towering 27 m (90 ft) campanile shown here was dismantled in 1983. St Bride's Church, East Kilbride, UK, 1963, Gillespie, Kidd & Coia

Distinctive for its wave-like form, this church was built predominantly for holidaymakers visiting Germany's North Sea coast. Clad in dark grey bricks, it replaced a 1960s construction that had become run-down by the testing coastal conditions.
St Marien, Schillig, Germany, 2012, Königs Arkitekten

◀ Better known for building handsome country houses for the well-heeled, Lutyens found himself working on this social housing project after his client, the Duke of Westminster, stipulated that he would donate the land if Lutyens would design the buildings. The striking chequerboard facades give scale to what might otherwise seem an overwhelming site. Grosvenor Estate, London, UK, 1930, Sir Edwin Lutyens

Comprised of three individual towers, these brick-clad apartment buildings half surround a similarly coloured 1930s bullring. Held in visual tension, each of the three buildings is formed of an extruded and stepped curved form that gives their inhabitants multi-directional views and generous terraces. Torres del Parque Apartment Buildings, Bogotá, Colombia, 1970, Rogelio Salmona

Best known for his Bilbao Guggenheim, Gehry designed this complex as three separate buildings, all made of concrete, but clad in white plaster, highly reflective stainless steel, and brick respectively. The form of each building gives the impression of leaning, fluid, or – in the case of the brick version – angular shapes. The buildings are linked by their arrangement and by the same window fittings.

Der Neue Zollhof, Dusseldorf, Germany, 1998, Frank Gehry

This fifteenth-century mosque has many precedents in the Asian sub-continent, but few match its balance and simplicity. Inside a network of heavy stone of columns lead to praying niches in the wall facing Mecca. Its name Sixty Dome is a curiosity since there are 77 domes – or 81 including the four corner towers. The moniker seems most likely to be a linguistic corruption from the Persian term for sixty pillars, which would reflect the number of columns inside. Sixty Dome Mosque, Bagerhat, Bangladesh, 1459

Aalto designed this concert hall for the Finnish Communist party for no fee, gaining in return complete creative freedom. He devised a specially rounded brick, almost square in plan, but narrower on one side, which allowed for a variety of wall curves – from gentle undulations to tight sculptural forms. Both examples can be seen here. House of Culture, Helsinki, Finland, 1958, Alvar Aalto

This intricately detailed 62 m (203 ft) high tower – with highly refined bands of ornate Arabic lettering and elaborate geometric patterning – has survived over eight hundred years despite being sited on the edge of a river and subjected to frequent earthquakes. Its survival is all the more extraordinary given that it probably marks the lost city of Firozkoh – destroyed by the Mongols in the 1220s. Minaret of Jam, Ghor Province, Afghanistan, 1174

This modern building – in the midst of the fourth oldest college at Cambridge, founded in 1348 – provides accommodation for a hundred undergraduates, a dining room and a common room. The study bedrooms are arranged around the stepped courtyard, allowing natural light to pervade the spaces. The raised courtyard and these steps reference Aalto's Säynatsalo Town Hall, completed a decade earlier.

Harvey Court, Gonville & Caius College, Cambridge, UK, 1962, Leslie Martin and Colin St John Wilson

The repeating vertical forms at the perimeter of this church represent various ways of deflecting or otherwise controlling the flood of natural light into the building – as do the boxes on top. While working on the project Kahn wrote: 'A great building, in my opinion, must begin with the unmeasurable, must go through measurable means when it is being designed and in the end must be unmeasurable … But what is unmeasurable is the psychic spirit.'
First Unitarian Church, Rochester, New York, USA, 1969, Louis Kahn

Built in the fashionable Romanesque style, with faience (glazed terracotta) to protect the building from London smog, this museum facade incorporates an abundant collection of sculpted animals: extinct creatures are seen to the east of the main entrance, and living creatures to the west. Terracotta historically refers to moulded objects which have a similar composition to brick, but are larger. The materials used are usually more refined and the resulting piece fired to a higher temperature making it harder. Natural History Museum, London, UK, 1881, Alfred Waterhouse

The offset positioning of these bricks allows natural light to fill this vineyard fermentation room, while avoiding direct sunlight. Off-site a computer-programmed robotic arm picked up each brick, added a line of mortar then accurately placed the brick to a predetermined design, which depicts a basket of grapes. Winery Gantenbein, Fläsch, Switzerland, 2006, Gramazio & Kohler Architekten and Bearth & Deplazes Architekten

This newspaper headquarters and printing facility is in the Brick Expressionist style, which flourished in Northern Germany and the Ruhr during the 1920s. Somewhat in response to their Bauhaus contemporaries, who condemned decoration of any sort, the Brick Expressionists espoused a more characterful style of work. They used decoration, colour, and expressive forms to create work that was deliberately playful, beautiful, and full of references. Anzeiger-Hochhaus, Hanover, Germany, 1928, Fritz Höger

Nicknamed 'God's Power Station' by Berliners, this Brick Expressionist church is punctuated with dark clinker bricks. The ribbed walls add to a machine aesthetic which is more restrained than most projects during the period, including other works by Höger. Church at Hohenzollernplatz, Berlin, Germany, 1933, Fritz Höger

This complex of buildings in a burgeoning Yangzhou development area provides meeting spaces and a dining area for local residents and office workers. Bricks formed from the alluvial soil of the nearby Yangtze River give a deep red-coloured tint to the intentionally traditional vernacular forms of the pitched-roof buildings.
Three Courtyard Community Centre, Yangzhou, China, 2009, Zhang Lei

A rare surviving fragment of a Russian medieval palace, this decorative facade shows a romantic and feminine side to brick. The building now houses a museum dedicated to its former occupier, Prince Ivan Ivanovich, sometimes known as Dmitry Ivanovich, son of Ivan the Terrible. Prince Dmitri Palace, Uglich, Russia, 1480

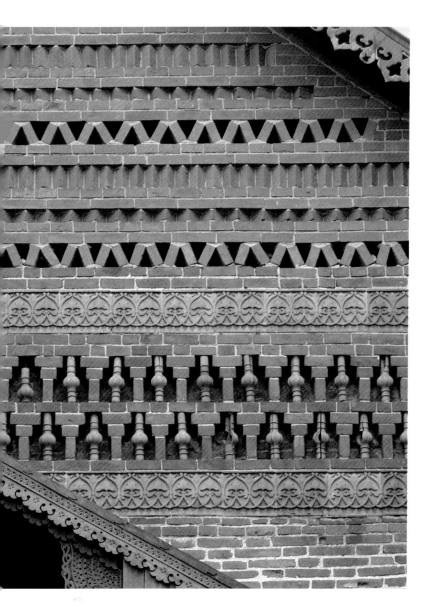

This is a functional building which is difficult to categorise stylistically, arriving as it did on the cusp of both Brutalism and Postmodernism; Stirling rejected both terms. The external form of the building expresses its internal functions. Lectures take place in the two bevelled blocks, revealing their ramped seating; workshops fill the top lit lateral ground floor spaces; and offices and laboratories fill the towers. One part of the building was required to be 30.5 m (100 ft) tall to provide a water tower with sufficient pressure for the hydraulic workshops beneath. Leicester University Engineering Building, Leicester, UK, 1963, Stirling and Gowan

This bulbous corner detail is typical of the highly individual and whimsical approach of the Amsterdam School which thrived between 1910 and 1930, and whose work was invariably in brick. Residents then and now enjoy the unique character of each apartment. Het Schip, Amsterdam, Netherlands, 1920, Michel de Klerk

Gropius built this factory eight years before he founded the Bauhaus. Its simple forms, functional spaces, and lack of ornament anticipate the architectural output of the school. Of note is the dramatic curtain wall, which – in a very early example of the form – meets at a corner without any visible structure. Fagus Factory, Alfeld, Germany, 1913, Walter Gropius

157

LANDSCAPE

◀ This 78 m (256 ft) long tunnel forms part of a pathway following the course of a drainage ditch. The oval brick vault is self supporting and tall, avoiding the risk of claustrophobia. The Brusince stream still follows the same route, and is visible beneath a steel grate on one side of the path.
Deer Moat Pathway, Prague, Czech Republic, 2002, Josef Pleskot

Serving a rural population this low-cost building was intended as a template for further public buildings. Bricks were not part of the local vernacular, but were made and fired nearby, and the buildings subsequently constructed by local workmen who were trained on-site. Formed of a series of domes and arches, natural light enters via glass blocks and narrow gaps between arches.
Kaédi Hospital, Kaédi, Mauritania, 1989, ADAUA

While still a teenager, Salmona was invited to join Le Corbusier as a draftsman in his Paris office. On his return to Colombia he created a series of buildings which demonstrated his Modernist training combined with a rich sense of his own cultural heritage. For this complex tiered structure Salmona typically utilised the roof – which he called the fifth facade – to provide circulation. Biblioteca Distrital Virgilio Barco, Gauteng, Colombia, 2001, Rogelio Salmona

Sculptor James Wines designed nine sheds for the Best Products Company, each subverting the 'big box' form of warehouse stores. One featured a peeling facade, others had moving or out-of-scale elements. Each playfully challenged what or how such a building could be. Not everyone understood the conceit; shortly after the completion of Indeterminate Facade one confused passerby called the authorities to report serious hurricane damage. Indeterminate Facade, Houston, Texas, USA, 1975, SITE and James Wines

This vast pyramid is 700 m (2296 ft) long, 280 m (919 ft) wide, and 30 m (98 ft) tall, making it the largest adobe building in the world. Adobe is the Spanish word for mud brick. The building is on a site of 540 acres (218 hectares) surrounded by 26 other major pyramids and mounds. The structure had many purposes. Some burials took place here, but it is thought there were also ceremonial areas and places for cooking and textile manufacturing. A thousand years of erosion – in particular by the recurring El Niño weather phenome-non – continues to denude the fabric of the building. Huaca Larga, Tucume, Peru, 1000

Sited on an arid plateau, it is estimated that over 10,000 Buddhist stupas, temples and monasteries were built here between the eleventh and thirteenth centuries. Over 2,200 survive – sometimes the structure is simply a dome, sometimes it consists of receding tiered terraces. The Burmese government restored many of the buildings in the 1990s but drew wide-spread condemnation from historians and preservationists for inauthentically repairing them. Consequently UNESCO has refused to recognise it as a World Heritage Site.

Ancient Temples of Bagan, Bagan, Burma (Myanmar), c.1000–1200

◀ The Robie House is a late and refined example of Wright's Prairie Houses. Intended to evoke the indigenous American landscape, Wright determinedly eschewed traditional architectural styles. Instead, inspired by the vast, flat and treeless plains of the American Midwest, his Prairie Houses are characterized by horizontal lines, and used local materials. Robie House, Chicago, Illinois, USA, 1910, Frank Lloyd Wright

This MIT student accommodation faces the River Charles. Its zig-zag shape allows for views up and down the river, and broke down the monotony of a large monolithic structure. The long facade is further broken up by the careful positioning of 'clinker' bricks, which are misshapen darkened bricks that are overheated during firing. Clinkers were often used by Arts & Crafts practitioners due to their uneven and seemingly handmade appearance. Baker House, Cambridge, Massachusetts, USA, 1949, Alvar Aalto

◀ Fired bricks envelop a structure of sun-baked bricks on this ancient ziggurat. Its pyramidal structure – with multiple flat terraces – is typical of the form. Once part of a bustling city of 50,000 people, this temple to Nanna, the Mesopotamian god of the moon, was originally topped by two further terraces, but these were unintentionally destroyed by locals and an overzealous English archaeologist in the 1850s. Ziggurat of Ur, Nasiriyah, Iraq, 2100 BC

Despite being one of the leading Modernists, Mies van der Rohe never dressed his buildings in concrete, the material of the movement. Instead, a series of country houses, such as these for a pair of industrialists, were clad in brick. Here the black frames and railings combine with dark brick to enhance a monolithic presence in the landscape. An internal steel frame allowed Mies to cut unprecedentedly large apertures, the glass of which could be retracted completely. Lange & Esters Houses, Krefeld, Germany, 1928, Ludwig Mies van der Rohe

This NGO in one of the poorest areas of Bangladesh offers training and support for local agricultural workers. Built on flood planes – and with the cost of raising the land prohibitive – the architects decided instead to build embankments around the site to protect it from flooding. The building features a collection of rooms, from large dining and training rooms to dormitories, a prayer room, and smaller more intimate spaces. All are quietly unified by the consistent use of locally hand-made bricks.
Friendship Centre, Gaibandha, Bangladesh, 2011, Kashef Mahboob Chowdhury/URBANA

◀ Kirkeby has been making brick artworks since 1965. This 15 x 9 m (49 x 30 ft) example in an Antwerp sculpture park has a rigorous 3 x 3 m (10 x 10 ft) grid. Each of the enclosed tower spaces have internal apertures, and the central pair also have external doorways. The experience of exploring the spaces echoes that of a walk in a labyrinthine Baroque garden. Untitled, Antwerp, Belgium, 1993, Per Kirkeby

Inspired by growth in the natural world, Utzon devised a unique approach to arranging architectural elements that he called 'Additive Architecture'. Each of the 63 sites in this development are square in plan, formed of an L-shaped house with a walled garden completing the square. Utzon described them as 'like flowers on the branch of a cherry tree, turning towards the sun'. This layering, and organic growth are also seen in Utzon's best known work, the Sydney Opera House. This view shows the Flemish bond which alternates stretcher and header along one course, with the following course offset so that the stretcher from one course sits directly in line with the header from the previous one. Kingo Houses, Elsinore, Denmark, 1959, Jørn Utzon

This industrial-scale room combines a garden with a series of platforms spiralling out from a central chimney. A frosted glass ceiling and one entire wall of glass facing parkland mean the space is permeated with light. The owner described how close to the landscape they felt from within: 'If a cloud goes over the sun, it's like turning off the light, if the wind blows, you hear the leaves, twigs falling on the roof, if it hails, you can't hear yourself think. It really is embedded in nature.' Featherston House, Melbourne, Australia, 1968, Robin Boyd

◀ Linking Saxony and Bavaria, and spanning the Göltzsch River valley, this 574 m (1883 ft) long viaduct is the largest brick bridge in the world. Bricks were made on-site where multiple brickyards produced 50,000 bricks per day. The total number of bricks used is estimated at over 26 million. The buildings surrounding it appear Lilliputian in comparison. Göltzsch Viaduct, Netzschkau, Germany, 1851, Johann Andreas Schubert

The versatility of brick is demonstrated in this sophisticated house, built on a restricted plot in west London. Sometimes the use of brick is austere and defensive, sometimes intimate – when they surround the bath for example. In all cases their application is confident and apposite. Brick House, London, UK, 2005, Caruso St John

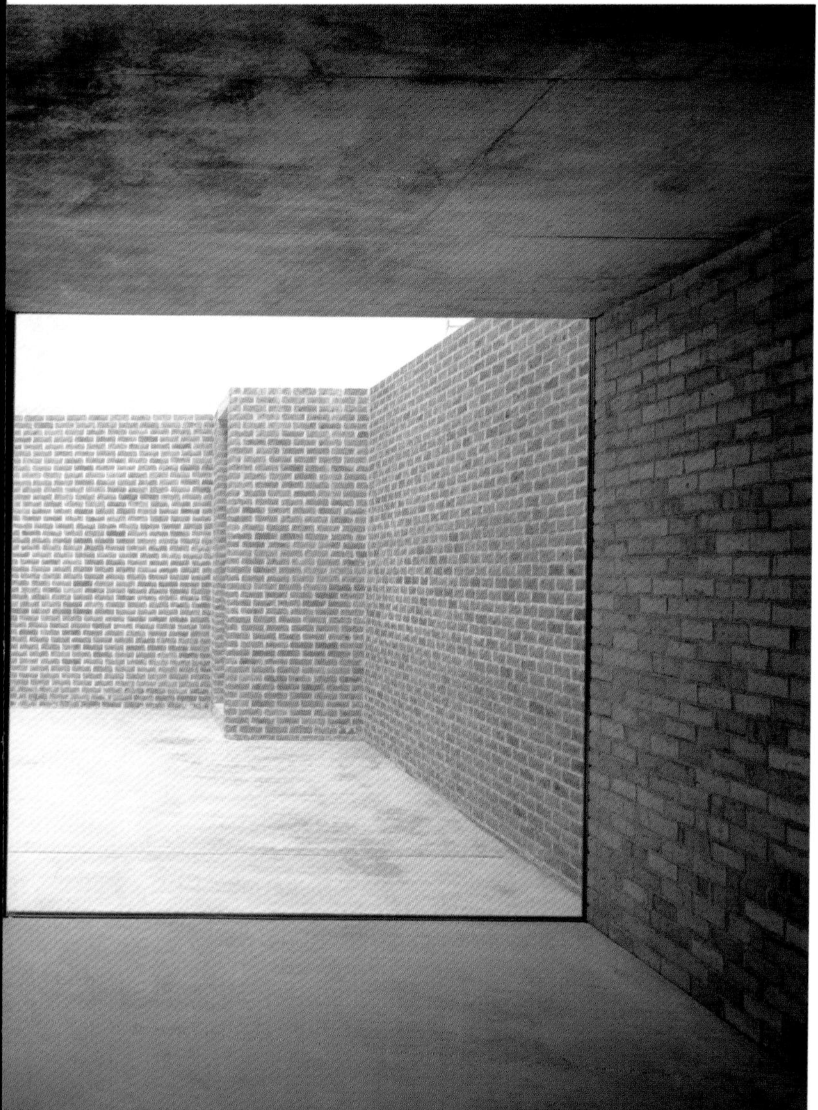

In the grounds of an eighteenth-century manor house these brick additions provide space for stables, an orangery, a swimming pool and related outbuildings. Coloured to match neighbouring roofs, the project demonstrates that carefully selected bricks can have all the refinement and elegance of more majestic materials.
Orangery and Stables, Geneva, Switzerland, Charles Pictet, 2008, Charles Pictet

These artists' studios and exhibition spaces are on the site of a former textile factory. To renovate the building and retain a sense of its industrial past, architects 51N4E kept much of the surviving structure. The new elements comprise of two pentagonal spaces. These tie the building together both in terms of infrastructure, and in terms of identity – as shown in this open-air entrance 'pavilion'. Buda Art Centre, Kortrijk, Belgium, 2012, 51N4E

This summerhouse in the hills of northeast Spain has many unconventional outdoor spaces, including this theatrical sheltered corner. The disparate room-like spaces are united by the consistent use of brown brick, while the swimming pool is tiled in a striking blood red. Family House, Girona, Spain, 1973, Ricardo Bofill

LIGHT

◀ Effortlessly simple, yet timeless rather than modern, this ethereal pale brick aisle is bathed in light. Although designed in 1913, and inaugurated in 1927, the building's completion was delayed following the architect's death in 1930. It was eventually completed in 1940 by the architect's son, the virtuoso furniture designer Kaare Klint. Grundtvig's Church, Copenhagen, Denmark, 1927, Peder Vilhelm Jensen-Klint

Dealing with primitive construction equipment and unskilled workers, Mashhadmirza kept the design very simple for this private house in one of the poorest areas of the city. The brick screen was inspired by *mashrabiya* (traditional Arabic screened windows) to provide privacy and shade in the Tehran heat. Brick Pattern House, Tehran, Iran, 2011, Alireza Mashhadmirza

Briefed to block noise and direct sunlight while retaining some light and ventilation, Anagram conceived this elegantly arranged perforated wall. It screens an office building for a human rights NGO. South Asian Human Rights Documentation Centre, New Delhi, India, 2005, Anagram

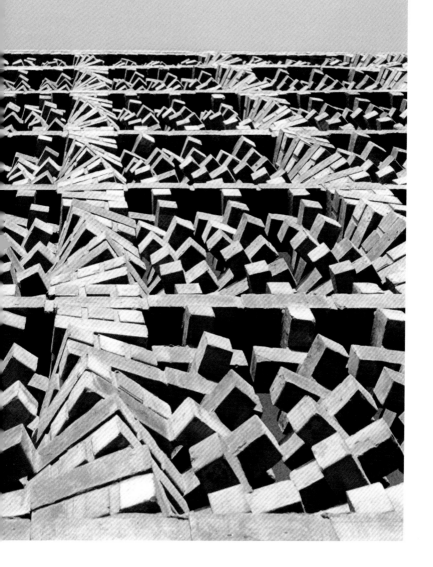

Baker was interested in developing economical, efficient, and sustainable vernacular buildings using local materials. Born in England, he moved to India in 1945 and stayed until his death in 2007. Bricks were central to his oeuvre, often incorporating perforated screens to promote air flow and to soften strong daylight.
Centre for Development Studies, Trivandrum, India, 1971, Laurie Baker

Mijares Bracho built homes, offices, and a series of ecclesiastical buildings in his native Mexico, each developing on his brick theme. This tiered arch motif became a trademark detail, which was sometimes also expressed externally. San José, Jungapeo, Mexico, 1982, Carlos Mijares Bracho

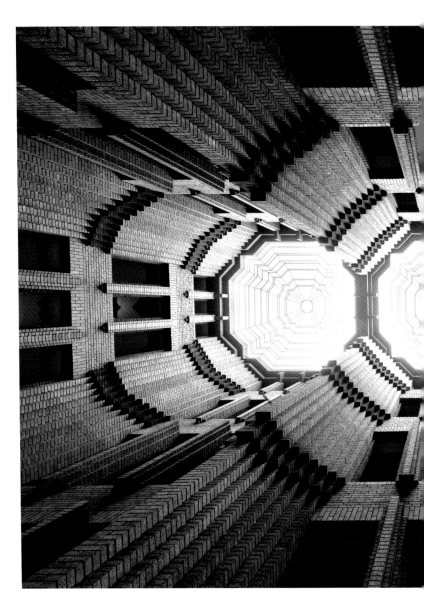

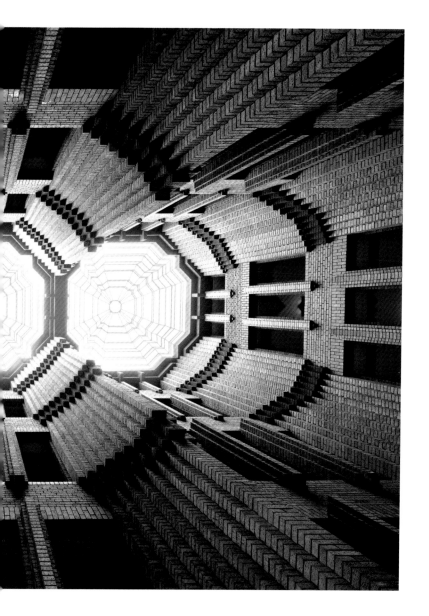

◀ Behrens is best known for his work for AEG from 1907, including the famous Turbine Factory, a logo, and product design. During this period his office assistants included architects who would become significant in the subsequent decades – Mies van der Rohe and Le Corbusier among them. This remarkable building for a dyeworks, built some years later, demonstrates an extraordinary attention to detail throughout. The centrepiece is this five-storey cathedral-like entrance hall, its apparently hanging coloured bricks bringing to mind the dyeing process. Technical Administration Building of Hoechst AG, Frankfurt, Germany, 1924, Peter Behrens

Conceived by Fidel Castro and Che Guevara in 1961, Cuba's National Art Schools were never fully completed, and much of the site on the outskirts of Havana is now abandoned. American embargoes meant that concrete was exorbitant and difficult to source so locally produced brick and terracotta were used. Those materials, and the landscape of a former country club, were exploited to produce a range of sprawling low-level buildings of intense dynamism and energy. School of Music, Havana, Cuba, 1965, Vittorio Garatti

This temporary pavilion was constructed over a wooden formwork using a technique known as a timbrel vault. The first layer of brick rests on the formwork and is mortared together. A subsequent layer or layers are laid on top, creating a tensile strength approaching that of reinforced concrete, and allowing the wide spans and rolling curves seen here. Bricktopia, Barcelona, Spain, 2013, Map13

◀ Following a visit by Pope John Paul II in 2003, this significant pilgrimage site, part of a monastery, was expanded to accommodate the increasing number of visitors. The multi-use hall is clad in slim terracotta tiles. The pixelated apertures bring light into the hall and break up the otherwise austere form. Pope John Paul II Hall, Rijeka, Croatia, 2010, Randi & Turato

These colossal arches are typical of Kahn's work on the vast 197 acre (80 hectare) site of the Bangladesh National Assembly. They are bold, geometric, and stately, yet – perhaps by virtue of the choice of material – remain humble and protective despite their powerful presence. National Assembly Building, Dhaka, Bangladesh, 1982, Louis I. Kahn

This powerfully austere space is brought to life by the skylights, and by the massive cylindrical void, which spans 5 m (16 ft) across the internal window surround. The aperture serves to highlight the site-specific sculpture by Erik Heide. Ravnsbjerg-kirken, Aarhus, Denmark, 1976, C. F. Møller Architects

◀ Built by the Great Northern Railway as their London terminus this solid and simple facade expresses the train sheds beyond and evokes the dependable majesty of Victorian viaducts and bridges. While the Kings Cross building is in the spirit of the Industrial Revolution, just twenty years later its neighbour, St Pancras, appeared in the form of a Gothic château. Kings Cross Station, London, UK, 1852, Lewis Cubitt

Software was required to create the watery design for these walls, and it had been intended that it would be constructed by robotic arm. In the end that proved too expensive and a local team of bricklayers became responsible for the hugely complex design featuring nine differently sized bricks. Lanxi Curtilage, Chengdu, China, 2011, Archi Union Architects Inc

Stepped brickwork defines the perimeter and roof of this striking family house in South Korea. The clients wanted a friendly building that welcomed the local community to share the space outside their home. Pixel House, Gyeonggido, South Korea, 2003, Mass Studies and Slade Architecture

Perforations allow air and city noise to permeate the walls of this museum. A typical house brick measures 21.5 × 10 × 6.5 cm (8½ × 4 × 2½ in). These specially manufactured grey bricks measure just 4 cm (1½ in) high, but some are as long as 53 cm (21 in). Colour matched mortar gives the building a solid, grounded quality.
Kolumba Art Museum, Cologne, Germany, 2010, Peter Zumthor

As well as contributing strength the form of this sinusoidal wall provides an exhilarating play of light throughout the day, especially outside, but also inside where stained glass colours the walls. Church of Christ the Worker, Atlántida, Uruguay, 1958, Eladio Dieste

Locally produced earthenware pots were embedded in the concrete ceiling of this library building in West Africa. The intense daytime heat is moderated by the small apertures, while the thick brick walls – with the same clay origins as the pots – contribute to the same goal. School Library, Gando, Burkina Faso, 2013, Diébédo Francis Kéré

Erik Gunnar Asplund and Sigurd
Lewerentz created Stockholm's
Woodland Cemetery between
1915 and 1940. It is now a UNESCO
World Heritage Site and an acknowl-
edged architectural masterpiece.
Into this landscape Celsing placed
his commission winning 'stone in
the forest', a new crematorium.
This immaculate and solemn barrel-
vaulted space is where mourners
encounter the deceased in a coffin
positioned at the centre of the room.
The New Crematorium, Stockholm,
Sweden, 2013, Johan Celsing

MASS

◀ This five-storey office building features what the architect has coined an 'architectural mountain'. The switch-back staircase reaches the top of the building in five flights arriving at the roof terrace 'summit'. Most captivating are the perforated walls witnessed en route, which allow views out, yet from afar give the building a resolute mass. ABC Building, Seoul, South Korea, 2012, Wise Architecture

Shoosmith worked for Sir Edwin Lutyens on the sprawling Viceroy's House elsewhere in New Delhi before designing this church for British troops stationed here. Echoing yet simplifying Lutyens' approach, the church has a fortress-like appearance, with few windows and an austere stepped form. Garrison Church of St Martin, New Delhi, India, 1930, Arthur Gordon Shoosmith

In stark contrast to his organic and undulating Einstein Tower of 1921, and perhaps inspired by a tour of Brick Expressionism in the Netherlands, Mendelsohn's Hat Factory is a linear, though no less dynamic industrial form. The tall elements represent industrial structures, while the horizontal ones contain administrative offices. Steinberg Hat Factory, Luckenwalde, Germany, 1923, Erich Mendelsohn

Höger followed the success of Chilehaus with this nine-storey office building on a neighbouring site. Every facade is covered in a diamond shaped pattern of hard-fired bricks and terracotta bosses, which represent themes of industry. Sprinkenhof, Hamburg, Germany, 1927, Fritz Höger

The design for this seventeen-storey tower was calculated as the highest feasible for masonry construction. It required walls that are 46 cm (18 in) at the top and 1.8 m (6 ft) wide at the base. The Monadnock Building was the swansong for monumental load-bearing masonry construction, which was replaced by steel and reinforced concrete. Its clean lines – inspired by a client driven by a sometimes related passion for simplicity and economy – produced a building of clarity and confidence. Monadnock Building, Chicago, Illinois, USA, 1891, Burnham and Root

◀ After a deluge destroyed a city in the area in 1532, a walled plateau was built on a rocky outcrop and all new buildings were constructed on it. With neighbouring areas vulnerable to flooding residents had no choice but to build upwards to accommodate a burgeoning population. Hence the isolated mud brick skyscrapers, many seven or eight storeys high – the tallest buildings of their kind in the world. Old Walled City of Shibam, Shibam, Yemen, 300

This seventeen-storey office is based on a cluster of cube modules measuring 6 x 6 m (20 x 20 ft). The recessed entrance and a public passage through the building help to diffuse the monolithic mass of most large scale corporate structures. Its pixelated form inspired one gamer to create a Minecraft version. DNB Bank Headquarters, Oslo, Finland, 2012, MVRDV

There has likely been a church on this site for over a thousand years. While parts of its medieval incarnation survive, most of the site was destroyed during World War II. Zumthor chose to incorporate the surviving elements, combining the dispersed original buildings into a coherent whole. Kolumba Art Museum, Cologne, Germany, 2010, Peter Zumthor

These informally arranged houses challenge the convention of terraces by taking advantage of the shared in-between spaces, and encouraging interaction between residents of this upmarket Tokyo suburb. The long red bricks were coloured white prior to firing, resulting in a pale pink tone.
Seijo Town Houses, Tokyo, Japan, 2007, Kazuyo Sejima

Grouped around a courtyard, this Dominican centre incorporates a chapel, rectory, nursery school, and a care centre. Meticulously detailed, the heavily grounded and sculptural form offers respite and sanctity – both literal and metaphorical – from a colourful and frenetic location.
Dominikuszentrum, Munich, Germany, 2008, Meck Arkitekten

Standing in the groves that are the reason for its being, this olive oil factory is split in two, with the larger agricultural side housing machinery and vehicles, and the smaller side housing production facilities and a tasting room. Agricultural Pavilion, Santurde, Spain, 2009, Barcena y Zufiaur Arquitectos

Built to serve a growing local population, Celsing won the commission for this complex, which includes a bell tower and assembly room, by competition in 1952. Made from hard-fired bricks – fired to a higher temperature for superior strength and heat resistance – and with few windows, the buildings have a weighty presence. Härlanda Church, Göteborg, Sweden, 1958, Peter Celsing

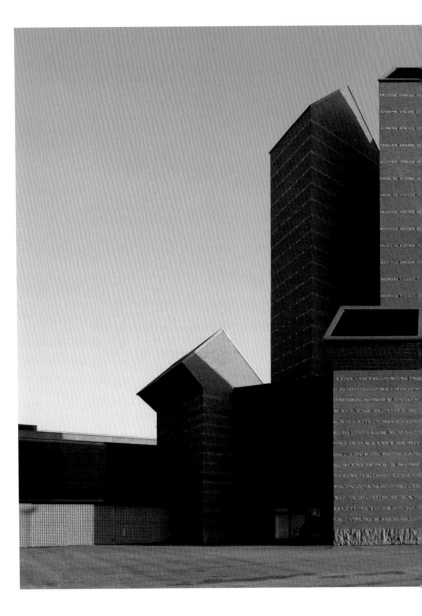

◀ Built on the site of a former industrial area, this arresting church was built to accommodate a new congregation of residents and to gather parish spaces and services that were formerly spread across the city. Its seven towers are 35 m (115 ft) high and their form reflects the sites' heritage as a former steelworks. Santo Volto, Turin, Italy, 2006, Mario Botta

Brick, like concrete, is strong in compression and weak in tension. This large sloping cantilever, which accommodates an auditorium, could only be achieved by cladding a reinforced concrete structure in brick.This is not a natural condition for bricks to be in, and this contributes to the building's unusual presence. University of Bremerhaven, Bremerhaven, Germany, 2011, Kister Scheithauer Gross

A pair of tower blocks, one an office (shown here), the other residential, assert themselves together and apart. The strikingly extruded facade features a vivid graphic colour treatment that breaks up the scale of the towers, and alludes to the shadows of neighbouring buildings. Amsterdam Symphony, Amsterdam, Netherlands, 2009, Cie Architecten

The grouped blocks of this monumental yellow brick building are arranged asymmetrically, yet their vertical and horizontal volumes are carefully composed to give balance and tension to the overall work. Influenced by Frank Lloyd Wright, and by the Brick Expressionists who had been active in Amsterdam, Dudok commissioned the overly long bricks especially and also designed much of the furniture and interior. Hilversum Town Hall, Hilversum, Netherlands, 1931, Willem Dudok

This is the tomb of Isma'il Samani, a Persian who ruled the city of Bukhara in the ninth and tenth centuries. The building is distinguished by quality of construction and craftsmanship, which was previously unseen. The lower part of the mausoleum lay under 2 m (6½ ft) of sediment for centuries until a Russian archaeologist excavated the site in 1934. Samanid Mausoleum, Bukhara, Uzbekistan, 943

This student accommodation is part of a 65 acre (26 hectare) campus university. Kahn's geometric constructions have the grandeur and presence of Classical antiquity, but their pure forms give them a timeless – even an unplaceable – quality. A plan grid tilted to 45-degrees affects much of the campus, as here, resulting in an unconventional and striking form. This image reveals the maintenance sometimes required in very damp environments: the bricks have been patched several times in just a few decades.

Indian Institute of Management, Ahmadabad, India, 1974, Louis Kahn

◀ 'A brick box with a concrete lid,' was how Holden modestly described this style, but his Machine Age stations set the architectural tone of London Transport for decades. They encapsulated the excitement for the future of transport while acknowledging the brick built suburban vernacular within which they were situated.
Arnos Grove Underground Station, London, UK, 1932, Charles Holden

The first of fourteen London 2012 buildings to be completed, this electrical substation supplied electricity to the Olympic Park and neighbouring Stratford City development. The 80 m (262 ft) long structure contains transformers and cooling apparatus in two towers, which are joined in a single storey that contains the switch room. Black bricks reference many local buildings that have similar coloured masonry or painted bricks. The building's aesthetic also promotes a sense of efficacy and dependability.
Primary Substation, London, UK, 2010, NORD Architecture

In the exposed environment of a former shipyard, this office and stockroom has a fortified exterior, with a scattering of appropriately hard metallic brick. Unusually, the building is designed by a team of graphic designers – long-term collaborators of the client. The result has a refreshing visual clarity. Fort Cortina, Amsterdam, Netherlands, 2011, Karelse & den Besten

PRESENCE

◀ Built by a local industrialist who made his fortune mining and exporting saltpetre (potassium nitrate) from Chile, this ten-storey office building originally served as a shipping headquarters. Appropriate to its purpose and proximity to the docks, the building is famed for its sharply angled ship's prow and deck-like tiered upper balconies. Chilehaus, Hamburg, Germany, 1924, Fritz Höger

FAT Architecture balanced their client's brief for innovative architecture with the residents' desire for traditional homes by playfully combining both requirements. The carefully chosen materials and pragmatic underlying plan somehow conquer the project's potential to be kitsch. Islington Square, Manchester, UK, 2006, FAT Architecture

Media personality Janet Street-Porter studied architecture with Piers Gough, founder of CZWG, and commissioned him to design this, her central London home. A series of exuberant interplays contribute to the characterful presence of the house, which Gough described as 'a kind of portrait' of the client. Log-shaped lintels top the windows, the diagonal grid of windows is continued into a metal trellis, and gradated brickwork in four shades give the building the appeal of a tea-dunked biscuit. Street-Porter House, London, UK, 1988, CZWG

This ten-sided tower was built more than one thousand years ago as a monument and memorial for a regional ruler. The cone makes up just under one third of the overall height of 53 m (174 ft). Its form illustrates an early example of geometry in innovative Islamic architecture.

Gonbad-e Qabus Tower, Gonbad-e Qabus, Iran, 1006

First used as a cargo dock on the
Leeds and Liverpool Canal in the late-
eighteenth century, Granary Wharf
recently became a centrepiece of
redevelopment in Leeds. Architects
Carey Jones took the surrounding
built heritage as a starting point for
their residential tower, which incorporates references to neighbouring
viaducts and railway arches. Candle
House, Leeds, UK, 2011, Carey Jones

Although incorporating an unprece-
dented amalgam of styles, Klint's
Expressionist church borrows heavily
from traditional Danish ecclesiastical
architecture, an example of which
is its crow-stepped gable. Built with
the same yellow brick inside and out,
the church stands in the centre of a
symmetrical housing estate – also
designed by Klint – which leads the
eye towards the heroic climax of
the church's monumental facade.
Grundtvig's Church, Copenhagen,
Denmark, 1927, Peder Vilhelm
Jensen-Klint

This pioneering social housing was built by a Socialist cooperative movement that encouraged workers to build their own properties using government loans. Far from being an icon of religious zeal, the spire is actually a secular equivalent – a proud architectural statement that communicates ownership and community. Het Schip, Amsterdam, Netherlands, 1920, Michel de Klerk

The last in a series of pre-war factories built along London's arterial Great West Road, Fletcher abandoned the whitewashed concrete and Egyptian faience of contemporaneous buildings to deliver gravitas in dependable brown brick. The symmetrical administrative block and central tower matches the format of much of the neighbouring modern architecture. The multi-storey frontage obscures a single-height top lit 'daylight' factory behind. Gillette Building, London, UK, 1937, Sir Banister Fletcher

Imbued with layers of symbolism, yet somehow lacking authenticity, Eisenman's first major public building is nonetheless an engaging early example of Deconstructivism. The fragmented brick forms reference a mock medieval armory building which was demolished after a fire to make way for the Wexner Center.
Wexner Center, Columbus, Ohio, USA, 1989, Peter Eisenman

This magnificent moated Tudor castle was built by Henry VI's Treasurer of the Household, Sir Roger Fiennes, who wanted a home appropriate to his position. Despite its great age it is an anachronism: the palace was designed to look like an ancient castle but its walls are not fortified.
Herstmonceux Castle, Hailsham, East Sussex, UK, 1441

◀ Sullivan's commitment to creating an authentic American style of architecture free from the Beaux-Arts tradition later inspired his more famous student, Frank Lloyd Wright. This building – the first of eight 'jewel box' banks, all of which survive, features elaborate decoration alongside its bold geometric form. National Farmer's Bank, Owatonna, Minnesota, USA, 1908, Louis Sullivan

In reference to the warehouses of the neighbourhood, this New York gallery has a brick facade though that is where the simularities end. The unusually long dark grey bricks are supplemented by a dark mortar, which helped create a monolithic exterior that one online commentator compared to 'a pixelated gorilla face'. Mortar is the generic name for any paste used to cohere masonry. Typically it is a mixture of sand, water and a binder such as cement. Gladstone Gallery, New York, New York, USA, 2008, Selldorf Architects

This uncompromising and somewhat inelegant residential building is by turns shyly introverted and defiantly assertive. The dark glazed brick demonstrates a quality of brick masonry rarely seen: its appearance is as urban and impregnable as exposed concrete. Duikklok, Tilburg, Netherlands, 2011, Bedaux de Brouwer

◀ Van der Laan was a Benedictine monk who designed only a handful of buildings, even fewer of which were actually constructed. His greater contribution was in thinking and writing about architectural space, and about systems of order. Those few structures that were built – such as this flawless church – successfully reinforce his theories. St Benedictusberg Abbey, Vaals, Netherlands, 1968, Dom Hans van der Laan

This 30 m (98 ft) high, domed church has an octagonal plan that allows sunlight to filter in throughout the day and illuminate its extraordinary Byzantine mosaics, for which it is better known. It is the only major church from this period to survive intact. Basilica of San Vitale, Ravenna, Italy, 547

Raymond Hood studied at the École des Beaux-Arts and worked as a draftsman until winning the internationally publicised competition to design Chicago's Tribune Tower. The American Radiator commission followed: Hood softened the form and Neo-Gothic references of his earlier work, but the black and gold colouring made the building just as dramatic. Not everyone was impressed: It is thought Ayn Rand's pitiful *The Fountainhead* character, Peter Keating, is based on Hood.
American Radiator Building, New York, New York, USA, 1924, Raymond Hood and John Mead Howells

This house forms part of a collection of buildings in the countryside outside the capital, Ougadougou. The wide eaves and a double-layered roof help promote cooling airflow. The site also features a school and a hospital, but its main role is as an arts venue and to cultivate and encourage the cultural awakening of the region. Opera Village, Laongo, Burkina Faso, 2013, Diébédo Francis Kéré

Given the task of creating a sense of place on the edge of a city, Rossi took the standard single-storey shed and added a cluster of towers – the scale of which is far in excess of the requirements for the heating and ventilation systems they hide. Proudly emblazoned with the store's name, the ceramic lettering brings to mind Italian public buildings of an earlier generation. Centro Torri Shopping Centre, Parma, Italy, 1988, Aldo Rossi

The Bukhara mosque has been completely rebuilt several times since the twelfth century, but this astonishing minaret – banded with ornamental brick – has survived intact for nearly nine hundred years. Legend has it that when Genghis Khan's army sacked the city in 1220, Kahn was so taken with the tower that he ordered it to be spared. Kalyan Minaret, Bukhara, Uzbekistan, 1127, Bako

Lutyens' monument is a memorial for over 70,000 lost British and South African men who died at the Battles of the Somme in World War I. It was originally built with French bricks, but in 1973 was refaced with English equivalents from Accrington. With a combination of latent power and solemnity this triumphal arch made complex stands on 16 Portland stone piers. Thiepval Memorial, Thiepval, France, 1932, Sir Edwin Lutyens

Moscow's famous collection of onion domes is one of the most recognisable brick buildings in the world. While its form in brick is without precedent, it was probably inspired by Russian wooden vernacular ecclesiastical buildings. Almost all of the decoration comes from the elaborate brickwork – the rest from the non-brick forms, which were coloured in stages between the 1680s and 1848. St Basil's Cathedral, Moscow, Russia, 1561

SCALE

◀ This former copper smelting chimney is the tallest brick structure in the world at 178 m (585 ft) high. The base has an external diameter of 26.5 m (87 ft). Closed in 1980 the tower was saved from demolition by a local campaign group and is now part of a State Park. Anaconda Smelter Stack, Anaconda, Montana, USA, 1919

The Old City of Sana'a is one of the earliest continuously inhabited cities in the world with evidence of habitation up to 2,500 years ago. The fortified centre has more than 6,000 flat-roofed houses, which range from four to nine storeys high, many of which are 1,000 years old. The towers are typically decorated with fired bricks and white gypsum. Old City of Sana'a, Yemen

Apparently individual units of one to four floors high are clustered together in this eight-storey residential building near London's South Bank. Local nineteenth-century warehouses inspired the use of brick, which is used to define each of the units – though the changing materials are a visual conceit rather than a representation of the underlying structure. Bear Lane, London, UK, 2009, Panter Hudspith

This near featureless facade hides a small scale physical prototype of Wright's famous Guggenheim spiral. Challenged by the client as to the absence of a shop window, Wright responded: 'We are not going to dump your beautiful merchandise on the street, but create an arch-tunnel of glass … seeing the shop inside with its spiral ramp and tables set with fine china and crystal, they will suddenly push open the door, and you've got them!' V.C. Morris Gift Shop, San Francisco, California, USA, 1948, Frank Lloyd Wright

This distinctive and expressive church was built for the growing community of a suburb of Aarhus, Denmark's second largest city. Its asymmetric facade features a 5 m (16 ft) diameter window and a deep fissure, which demarcates the bell tower from the main church building. This image clearly shows English bond – a very common type of bonding where a course (a single layer of horizontally laid bricks) of stretchers alternates with a course of headers. Ravnsbjerg-kirken, Aarhus, Denmark, 1976, C.F. Møller Architects

This stolid apartment block sits on an artificial island that was built as a wave breaker for the Amsterdam docks. Deliberately referencing the local industrial vernacular, the building was built in brick. The windows are subtly offset by half a brick. This device is almost imperceptible, but is enough to diminish the monotony of a grid at this scale. Langhaus, Amsterdam, Netherlands, 2000, Diener & Diener

These tiered clusters add drama and an organic, almost mountainous presence to the River Thames water-side in Docklands, east London. They are particularly distinguished when compared against their neighbours, a mixture of handsomely proportioned salvaged warehouses and banal, mediocre Postmodernist apartments. Free Trade Wharf, London, UK, 1987, Holder Mathias Alcock

A travertine cathedral stood on this site from 1080. When a new cathedral was proposed using the rediscovered invention of brickmaking (which had curiously died out with the Romans) it was decided to build around the existing cathedral, which wasn't destroyed until 1225. Although planned to be in the Romanesque style, the building became predominantly Gothic in accord with the prevailing ecclesiastical architectural style of the late-twelfth century. As a result, it is the first Gothic cathedral to be built of brick, and was influential in the spread of the Brick Gothic style throughout Northern Europe. Roskilde Cathedral, Roskilde, Denmark, 1170 – 1405

The largest brick building in Europe, this monumental coal-fired power station was built to supply the power needs of central and southern London. Its industrial Art Deco base is topped by fluted classical columns, which house chimneys. The architect also designed Britain's famous red telephone box, and the later Bankside Power Station, 1947, now Tate Modern.
Battersea Power Station, London, UK, 1934, Sir Giles Gilbert Scott

◀ This basilica was built by the Roman Emperor Constantine and was probably initially used as a throne room. The vast hall is the largest surviving from antiquity, with huge internal dimensions of 67 × 27 m (219 × 88½ ft), and with a ceiling some 33 m (108 ft) high. Basilica of Constantine, Trier, Germany, 310

This 105 m (344 ft) long ziggurat is 25 m (82 ft) high in its ruined state, but was once twice that height. The extant materials – mud brick (beneath) and fired brick (on the surface) – are original and were revealed in excavations from 1935 onwards, after oil prospectors saw the site from the air. Mud bricks are created from a mixture of sand (or soil or silt depending on the location), clay and water, and a fibrous binding element such as straw, sticks or manure. An open frame is filled with the mixture. When set the frame is removed and the mud brick left to dry for several hours. Tchogha Zanbil, Khuzestan Province, Iran, 1250 BC

This vast and formerly lavish imperial bathhouse was free and open to the public, who could enjoy gardens, a library, and an Olympic size swimming pool on the 9000 m^2 (96875 sq ft) site. Built in four years, estimates suggest there were 4,000 bricklayers amongst the 15,000 strong workforce. Fully functional for over three hundred years, the baths were constructed in brick, but clad in marble and mosaics internally, and lined with stucco on the exterior.
Baths of Caracalla, Rome, Italy, 216

Poelzig's series of brick factory buildings were linked by railways. Factories offered architects of the early twentieth century an opportunity to formulate a new typology – to decide how industrial buildings should look. Poelzig's Expressionist design distinguished load-bearing and non load-bearing bricks with different shaped windows – those with Roman shaped arches were load-bearing. The overly large crow-stepped gable is another visual device. Milch Chemical Factory, Luboń, Poland (then Germany), 1911, Hans Poelzig

This moated courtyard is neighbour to an eighteenth-century cemetery that required expansion. Monestiroli created this three-sided ceremonial entrance, which incorporates several thousand tombs – each represented by a white stone panel organised in a grid around the perimeter. Brick provides a benign and softening counterpoint to the austere and repetitive stone plaques. Cimitero Maggiore, Voghera, Italy, 1995, Antonio Monestiroli

This is the earliest surviving mill in Manchester, and part of Murrays' Mills, a steam powered cotton production plant. The mill stands on the Rochdale Canal, which from 1804 provided access for the delivery of raw cotton and coal to power the mill, and to distribute the manufactured fine cotton. The mill had a workforce of 1,000 people and remained in operation for 150 years. Old Mill, Manchester, UK, 1798

Occupying an immense site in the centre of Bukhara, this massive fortress covers almost 10 acres (4 hectares), its walls rising to 20 m (66 ft). The age of the structure has not been accurately established, but it is thought to have been the residence of local rulers from at least the year 500. The Ark, Bukhara, Uzbekistan, 500

One of the tallest ancient structures in the world, this stupa is 122 m (400 ft) high. Formed of 93.3 million bricks and with foundations that are 8.5 m (28 ft) deep, it is estimated the building took fifteen years to complete. A house brick is made almost entirely of clay as it is found in the ground. After processing the bricks are fired at around 1000°C (1800°F). The chemical composition of brick clay is typically 60 per cent silica, 30 per cent alumina, 8 per cent iron oxide, and small elements of lime and magnesia. In contrast the bricks in this stupa are mixed with fine sand resulting in a greater compressive strength. Jetavanaramaya, Anuradhapura, Sri Lanka, 273–301

One of the most influential buildings in the world, the Wainwright Building became a template for the skyscraper. Sullivan created the tripartite form which echoes that of a classical column: its solid base incorporated street-facing spaces, its shaft was repeated to the required height, topped with a cornice to complete the building visually. Despite the conceptual allusion to Classical form, the decoration eschews such references. Wainwright Building, St Louis, Missouri, USA, 1891, Louis Sullivan

This massive museum of Chinese history uses salvaged local materials of various shapes, sizes, and materials. Shu deliberately alluded to both the topography of the area by making mountainous references, and to the sea-trading tradition of Ningbo: the building's object-like autonomy and boat prow form make it seem like a giant vessel floating through the landscape. Ningbo Museum, Ningbo, China, 2008, Wang Shu

Combining elements of a town hall, a nineteenth-century school, and a 1990s storage building, the architects unified a patchwork of brick into a new whole. The existing elements are decipherable, which means the renovation has a palpable sense of both history and rebirth that is appropriate to its role as a community centre. Community Centre Westvleteren, Westvleteren, Belgium, 2011, Atelier Tom Vanhee with Room & Room

▶ Built by successive Chinese Empires to dissuade and obstruct invaders, this series of walls – the longest man-made structure on earth – cumulatively measures over 21,000 km (13,000 miles). Only walls from the later Ming dynasty (1368–1644) are built in fired brick. Earlier constructions consist of rammed earth, stone, and mud brick. Great Wall of China, China, 300 BC–1644 AD

Index and Glossary

Endnotes

p7   Barker, Paul, 'Architecture: Hush now…',
     The Independent, 25 September 2014
p27 Heyer, Paul, 'Architects on Architecture',
     New Directions in America, The Penguin
     Press, 1967. p41
p139 Green, Wilder, Louis I. Kahn, *Architect*,
     Museum of Modern Art, 1961
p182 Vila, Tono. 'Interview with Jørn Utzon',
     Quaderns d'Arquitectura i Urbanisme, 157,
     April–June: Barcelona, 1983.
p184 Percival, Lindy. 'Robin Boyd: architectural
     rule book rewritten', *The Canberra Times*,
     5 June 2010
p270 Glancey, Jonathan. 'An architecture free
     from fads and aesthetic conceits'
     The Guardian, 16 October 2007
p278 *Survey of London, Volume XLVI, South
     and East Clerkenwell*, Yale University Press,
     2008. p174
p296 Waltering, Adam, *ArchDaily*, 14 June 2011
p323 Goldberger, Paul, 'High-Tech Emporiums',
     The New Yorker, 25 March 2002

Phaidon Press Limited
Regent's Wharf
All Saints Street
London N1 9PA

Phaidon Press Inc.
65 Bleecker Street
New York, NY 10012

phaidon.com

First published 2015
© 2015 Phaidon Press Limited
This edition first published 2019
© 2019 Phaidon Press Limited

ISBN 978 0 7148 7855 3

A CIP catalogue record for this book
is available from the British Library
and the Library of Congress.

Commissioning Editor: Emilia Terragni
Project Editor: Taahir Husain
Production Controller: Adela Cory
Design: William Hall

Printed in China